Fishing Magic: A Texas Bass Handbook

Roland Carroll

Table of Contents

Introduction

In this book I will lay out as many sound hints and tactics as I feel are important to making your bass fishing on our lakes more productive. I will not be quenching your artistic inner self with overly descriptive writings. I won't be using an entire paragraph to describe the rising of the early morning sun or the beautiful shimmer on the water. We will cover bass fishing with a no-fluff, just-a-facts-only style of approach. So if an artistic read is what you crave, this isn't the book for you. As in the last Fishing Magic book, this handbook is full of good and useful information without the fluff.

The largemouth Bass is probably one of the most popular targets for anglers other than the catfish, and is one of the toughest game fish to pattern and figure out. This sought after sport fish changes its patterns on a daily basis, making it very hard to stay on top of it from day to day. Once you think you have a pattern figured out, the fish changes its habits and vacates the area and seems to have simply disappeared. Many times, much to your grief, the fish seem to never visit the honey hole you have found again. It appears sometimes that you will find an aggressive school of fish willing to hit any lure you throw at them, and then no matter how many times you check that spot, you can never find those fish there again. There are always reasons for this change in the bass's behavior, and learning the habits of the fish can help you locate these same fish at another stopping point in their migrations, learning the links in the chain so to say.

The bass is affected by outside stimuli more than any other fish that I chase. It is as if the fish is designed to frustrate the angler at every turn. Things like changing water levels, along with changes in current, and weather conditions seem to have the ability to shut this fish down and turn them off of a previously found pattern. It takes more time than we usually have to adapt to these nerve-wracking changes in the fishes' behavior, and to increase the amount of fish we put in the boat. Most of the time, even though the fish have eased into an almost dormant state, they are still in the area and can still be coaxed into hitting your lures. So don't give up; learn to adapt as the fish changes, and increase the success you have. The available time you do have to spend with your electronics on your favorite lake is time well worth spending to further your knowledge of the travel routes that the bass use, thus letting you intercept them at more places.

The one thing that has helped me the most in understanding the non-active periods that bass go through is the time I spent fishing clear private lakes where I could take the time and watch the fish. As a kid I found this to be a treasure trove of useful information for me. Simply by watching the bass that I was after, I was opened up to a whole new way of judging their behavior and moods. Sometimes as I watched, I would notice a large fish sitting in a pocket of grass or on another type of structure and watch its behavior and actions as I presented lures to the fish. What I found was that the fish could be motivated into feeding or attacking an offering just out of aggression by presenting the bait to the fish time after time, enticing the fish to strike through sheer torment. Once a large bass was located sitting dormant in a pocket of grass, I would cast my small spinner bait time after time at the fish, bringing the lure right in front of her. I would cast past the fish and retrieve the bait so it would pass right in front of her as she sat motionless. On the first five or six casts, the fish would ignore the offering and pay no attention to the lure at all. Then, on the next few casts, the fish would start to change its posture and slowly start to show the lure a little more attention. After a few *more* casts, the bass started to become noticeably more aggressive to the lure and intently watched the lure more closely as it passed. Finally, after maybe a missed strike or two, the fish seemed to become highly irritated and would attack the bait as if she hadn't eaten in days. Sometimes this process took at least ten to fifteen casts to catch the fish I was targeting. Think about all of the times you were fishing heavy cover and finding the fishing to be a little slow. You probably wouldn't have had the patience to cast at that cover over and over again, maybe ten times or more, to get a fish to hit. You know from doing the leg work that fish are using that cover, but it is still almost impossible to spend the time needed to coax a fish into hitting your lure when you have so much more good looking water ahead of you to fish. I'm not saying that you cast at every piece of cover at least ten times, but if you know the fish are there, try to make an effort not to give up to fast. Many times just making a few more casts to a certain piece of cover is all it will take to catch a fish that you easily could have passed up. The act of making repetitive casts to good areas is one of the most important tactics that I learned by just watching the behavior of the bass I was targeting.

When chasing mature bass in shallow water, this is a very important tactic that you need to become more aware of to help you catch more of these mature fish, fish that you could easily pass up, not ever knowing that they were there. When you find that perfect lay down or any other good piece of cover, try to spend a little more time picking it apart; it could pay off with some solid bass.

Bass in shallow water are by far the fish most likely to be affected by outside influences, a lot more so than the fish staging in deeper water. When targeting fish in shallow water, you are at a huge disadvantage to start with. You have to deal not only with the influences of weather and water conditions, but also with the fact that these more mature fish are very spooky; your approach is hard for them to miss. You will have to figure out why these fish are in shallow water to begin with, why they are using the cover that they are on, and what advantage that cover gives them. To make all of your shallow water fishing more productive, you have to start in deep water and learn the movements of the bass, or should I say you need to find the sign posts and travel routes that lead the fish to shallow water. The reason a shallow water spot always seems to be productive to you is that there is a travel route from the deep water guiding the fish to this area. Fish usually don't feel safe in shallow water, and they want a quick retreat route to follow back into the safety of deep water. This understanding will eliminate a lot of wasted time when searching for bass in the abundant shallows in our lakes.

Bass are a school-oriented fish that have a school-oriented holding pattern that can be learned by the angler who will spend the time required to find the staging areas. This knowledge will help you to understand the reasons the fish move in and out of certain areas at certain times. To do this you will have to make a mental checklist to follow when you are out on the lake, and try to avoid fishing locations just because you have caught fish there in the past. Find the reason that you have caught fish there in the past; in other words, cover the area with your electronics, and find the travel route the fish are using to move into that area. After you find this travel route, you can find the other key spots on the route to catch fish that you were only catching when they came shallow. By spending a little time doing this, you can open up many more fish catching opportunities just by getting to know the surrounding area that you normally fish.

The greatest tool you have in increasing the numbers and the size of the bass you catch is your mind. Learn to harness your mind, and use it as the major asset it is in your fishing. When you are out on the lake, you have to know you will succeed in your quest and catch the numbers and size of the fish you are after. You have to start to use your mind as a tool—and what a tool it is. It is by far the greatest thing you have in your grasp, and it can make or break the success you have while out fishing. You have to learn to visualize the fish you are after moving in on your lure and to see the fish striking the bait in your mind. This important law-of-attraction aspect of fishing will be covered in a later chapter, but first we need to cover the type of areas in which to look for your quarry, the largemouth bass, so for now, learn to use the mind as a guide to help in the search for the deep water sanctuaries of the bass.

With today's wonderful electronics, along with all of the modern products we have at our disposal, there is no reason that the clue to the fishes' daily habits and movements can't be unlocked to allow us to put more fish in the boat. Learn to think out of the box when out on the lake; put yourself in the fishes' fins, so to speak. Try to visualize what it is that the fish is doing at a certain time or under certain circumstances and above all, know you will be rewarded greatly when you learn to know what she knows. It might sound funny to say "Be the fish," but it is the greatest thing you can learn to help you increase the amount of fish you catch. Have the confidence that you have a good idea of what the fish are doing and that this knowledge is going to reward you with a great day of fishing. Maybe instead of thinking that a day when you catch twenty- five fish is a good day, you might start to think of a day like that as a day when you didn't give your all when out on the lake. Set your standards high and, above all else, live up to these standards. Stop wondering if you are going to have a good day, and start knowing you will have a great day. Be the kind of fisherman you want to be by fishing the way you set out to fish and believing you will be rewarded for that plan.

A beautiful bass

Points

The first thing to do when starting your day on the lake is to decide what type of structure on which you want to start your search for bass. Whichever small area of the lake that you wish to start your daily search, you have got to treat this area as if it were a lake in itself. By this I mean dissect the area that you want to fish into a smaller version of the entire lake you are on. View a large cove as a lake in itself, with channels, points, and other structures just like a larger lake. Forget about the good shoreline you have caught fish on in the past; it's time to learn the bottom structure in that surrounding area and find out why the fish are in that area to begin with. There are a few easy-to-learn tactics that help you get to know how to approach your search for these schools of fish in your areas. Don't get in the habit of thinking that all your time on the lake needs to be spent casting your lures for bass. Spending time searching for the bass, and finding the more productive methods and places to catch them, will put more fish in the boat than just fishing your way to the fish. You have the electronics in your boat, so use them to your advantage to find the type of fishing you want to enjoy. Take the time need to explore, and don't think about the fish in the lake that are ready to be caught; it will be well worth it in the long run.

The first types of structure we are going to cover are the points that are in the area where you choose to start. During most times of the year, it is best to start with the main lake points of your lake and then move farther back in the creeks, checking each of the points as you go. Look at the surrounding shorelines to try to get an idea of what the topography of the bottom is like under the water simply by looking at what the topography of the land is above the water. When you find that point that has the right topography, or just looks right, start out by going over the point over and over with your electronics to get to know the contours and depth changes of that point. Start as shallow as you can, and work out toward deeper water. Zigzag back and forth over the point, moving out a little deeper on every pass. Take note of how the point drops off on each side. A sharp drop-off is going to be your best bet at holding bait and in turn the lurking fish. Follow the point out and find out where this drop-off goes. What you are looking for is a descending structure that will fall off into the lake's depths and has a travel route for the fish to follow onto the point. The spot where the crest of the drop-off descends down to the level of the thermocline is going to be the key area on that point, which is the spot the bait and bass are going to access to feed. It is important to have these few things going on to make this a point that is worth your repeated visits. A point that has a ledge or flat area at the level of the thermocline is going to be much more productive, especially if there is some cover at these spots. Once you find the connection to the thermocline, found in most lakes at around twenty to twenty-five feet, you can journey up the point looking for the road signs and stopping off spots the fish will use on that point.

To find the thermocline in your lake, go out into deep water in the morning hours and search the depths with your electronics. The thermocline is usually visible on your graph, and most of the time you will actually see the shad holding at that depth. Whenever the structure you are fishing, no matter what that structure is, meets the thermocline, this will make that location more appealing to the bait and bass alike. A drop-off that has a crest or a ledge at that depth can really be a honey hole that can produce big bass for years.

Take the time you need to get to know the main lake points, and spend time on your electronics to find the travel routes the bass use on those points, and you will be rewarded with a year-round, bass producing location. The next step is to move off of the main lake to the secondary points and repeat this process to locate the travel routes from deep water onto the points farther into the cove. This process can be repeated all the way back into the creek to find the productive points in that cove. Think of the travel route as if it were a road map; the fish will set up on a certain defined location and will travel via road signs to the next location, and so on. These road signs might be as simple as an edge of a creek that cuts in close to a point, then a row of stumps ending near a rock pile, and then maybe onto a weed line at the shore. Just remember that fish are going to use a defined travel route to the areas they like to feed. These travel routes are the key that makes an area of shallow water able to produce good numbers of mature fish. Get to know the bottom structure of the points, and pinpoint the travel routes the fish are using. It is important that the fish have a defined roadway to access in any area you choose to fish. Most of those shallow water fishing spots you have confidence in, and always seem to catch a few fish at, will have a bass roadway leading into these areas from deeper water. This travel route is a certainty and needs to be explored for all that it has to offer. Cover the area from shallow water out to deeper water, and more times than not you can find spots along this route to catch these same fish on other structures other than just the shoreline.

As you move back into the feeder creek coves, you can still cover the points in the same manner that you covered the main lake points until the water becomes shallower than the thermocline. Fish will still use points in the shallowest of shallow water, but their travel routes to these points will be a little different, though still in the form of creek channels, stump rows, humps or ridges and weed lines. Instead of accessing the points from the thermocline, the fish will access the point from the safety of the creek channel. Remember as you move into the smaller back areas that points will still exist into the tightest of these areas. Sometimes these points will be in the form of a point created by weeds or brush jutting out from a grass line or brush line, but the fish will still use these points as ambush locations, just as they use the cover on the main lake points as ambush spots. Points seem to always play some kind of part in the way fish set up to ambush prey, so any time you notice a point of any kind, this might be an ambush spot that the bass use to feed.

When looking for the critical little things on the points that make them productive, don't be in a hurry to wet a line and start fishing. Spending time on your electronics will be worth it in the long run—the more time spent the better. When using your electronics over these areas, you will surely see bait fish and predators while you are searching. You will see balls of bait fish with the isolated arcs of predator fish relating to the ball, and waiting to feed on the suspended bait fish. You can spend a lot of time stopping and fishing all of the beckoning fish you find on your graph, but you will soon start to realize that, more often than not, these fish that looked so appealing will not hit your offerings. Learn to understand the fish you see on the screen of your electronics, and you will start to notice which bass are the fish that will be more willing to hit the lures you present. The first thing to find on your graph is the bait. Find the bait and you will find the bass. But just because you find a large school of bait fish with well defined arcs of predators lying in wait does not mean the bass you see are aggressive at that time. The bass is one of the finickiest fish I have every gone after. They will break your heart at times when you know the fish are there but they refuse to react to anything you present to them. Be patient, and sooner or later you will find them in a feeding mood.

When you locate a school of bait on structure, the main thing to look for is a school of bass that are in a feeding mode. This will be clear to you once you encounter it a few times. When bass are feeding on the bait present, the arcs of the bass on your graph will be a little more closely related to the school of bait, and will be relating to that bait at different depths. Remember that the main thing to look for in and around the bait is the lines of moving fish. By this I mean the line that is created on your graph when a fish is moving. Unlike the arc of a stationary fish, the mark of a feeding fish will appear as a line as the graph details the fish on the move. These fish are chasing bait and are in a feeding mode. These are the fish you will want to throw out a buoy on and drop a spoon on or bring your deep diving crank bait through to catch the bass while they are feeding. Probably the most consistent method I use for catching good numbers of big fish is to locate them in this manner and drop a large jigging spoon right in the middle of the school. The fluttering action of the spoon as you let it fall through the bait will attract a bass wanting to take advantage of a wounded shad. I say again it takes time on your electronics to understand the different behaviors of bass as they hold on bait fish, and to start to understand which bass will be more likely to hit a presented lure. The one drawback to fishing the open water schools of bass is the release factor. What I mean by this is that if you hook and then lose a bass out of the school, it will turn the feed off. The bass will stop hitting anything for at least twenty minutes. This is something that can drive you crazy when you finally locate a receptive school of bass. The case also applies when you are releasing bass back into the school. It is best to put these fish, if they are of legal size, in your live well and release them before you move to a new location. When this shutdown happens, it is best not to fight it. Just move to a different spot and return after the spooked fish have settled down. Don't try to force feed these fish; it will only spook them more since they already know something isn't right. Come back later to find faster action.

The schools of bass you see on the bait fish are the bass you want to encounter on the points as they travel up their travel routes to feed. You just have to spend the time to see which points will be the most appealing to the bass at that time. Learn to understand the travel patterns of the bass in your area and increase the amount of time you can catch these same fish.

Another nice bass

River and Creek Channels

The winding channels through our lakes are the most well defined natural highways that the bass can travel. These channels meander all through our favorite lakes and should be a place the fisherman becomes very familiar with. It will just take a little time with your electronics to see where on the channels the fish will be holding and the stepping off areas of these channels the bass use the most to enter shallower water. The stepping off points are the side roads the fish use to access other areas, especially shallow water. It is extremely important to become very familiar with the river and creek channels in the lake you fish.

The first place to start when concentrating on river and creek channels to locate bass is the time of year you are fishing. In the winter and summer months, I have no problem fishing the main river channel of a lake, many times fishing in water depths of thirty to fifty feet. Although fishing at these depths takes more concentration on the feel of the bait and the watching of the line, these deep water haunts can yield incredible catches of big bass. In mid-winter and summer, the main goal is to find the high traffic areas on the bends and forks of the river channel; when you find them, these high traffic areas can reward you with huge catches of mature fish. One of my favorite areas to key on at this time of year is the bluffs created by the river and creek channels, then finding the small ledges on these bluffs. These areas seem to really appeal to the big deep-water largemouth bass. You will find after closely looking at the edge of a bluff that there are many little ledges along the face to target. The majority of the time in this situation I will leave the jigging spoon in the boat, choosing to throw a heavy jig or a heavily weighted worm to get these burrowed-up bass to hit. I can slowly cover the ledge and spend more time in the sweet spot to coax a big fish into sampling my offering. One vital thing to remember when fishing this deep water tactic is how important boat control is. You will have to stay on the trolling motor to keep your line as straight as possible. Any bend in the line at this depth will make feeling the hits much more difficult, while making the hook set a little weak at times. You will have to stay in contact with the bait constantly to work the lure effectively in these tight areas. I do love fishing deep water above all other areas on a lake, but I know from experience that it's not for everyone. If you do your homework and learn the good deep water locations in the lake you fish, you might discover a whole new way of targeting the big fish we all want to catch.

In late winter and late summer, the bass will start to make the move back up the creeks to take advantage of more shallow water opportunities. We all know that in the spring the fish head shallow to reproduce, but in the late summer the bass will migrate up the creeks following the schools of shad that move into the shallows each fall. The intersections where the creeks meets the river channel can hold several schools of bass at a time; all of these fish are ready to make their move up the creeks and will stage in these locations to feed and grow fat. As winter starts to lose its grip and spring approaches, the bass will start a steady movement up the creeks, stopping at many key spots along the way. Distinct bends in the channels will hold these wanderers, giving them time to take advantage of the schools of bait that travel with them. The junctions where the main creek channel meets other creeks branching off are always good areas for holding transitioning fish at this time of year. Some fish will head up these intersecting creeks to preselected spawning flats, while others will continue onto spawning flats all the way to the back of the cove via the main creek channel. The areas where you have found spawning fish in the past need to be investigated thoroughly so you can find the travel routes the bass are using to enter that area. This knowledge will lead you to fish that can be caught before they branch off on the spawning flats.

Getting to know the way the creek lays out in its journey to the back of the cove is one of the more difficult tests you will undertake with your electronics. The actual way a creeks meanders along the lake bottom can play havoc on the mental perception of the creek's path you are creating in your head when trying to map out its course. At times you will have to crisscross and then circle the areas a few times before you get an idea of the true course of the creek. This is very important to do to get the most out of your fishing when targeting the creeks.

You will find out that as the creeks move shallower, you will have to key on the definite irregularities in the creek channels to intercept the moving bass. The fish use these spots as rest areas to feed on while waiting for the moon and weather to cooperate with their goal—to reproduce. These spots will hold the fish temporarily while they are on the move to their shallow spawning areas. When these fish reach the area in the creek channel that gives the best access to the spawning areas they choose, the fish will move out of the creek channel at a defined place and set up close to the creek before moving up to spawn. When located, these areas can be a bonanza for the heavier fish in the area. Although the fish really want to move up and will sometimes try several times to make that move, the security of the creek channel will draw them back each time there is a weather change or water level change that hampers their move shallow. There will be a point when conditions are right and nothing will keep the fish from moving up; at this point the fish are dead set on making their yearly bounty of babies. More often than not, this move is orchestrated by the males that have been preparing the way, and the females simply follow to complete the cycle.

There is one story that comes to mind when I think about the times I have taken advantage of the tactic of locating bass as they make their move from a creek to their spawning areas. A few years ago, my brother-in-law Gary and I were heading out to fish on Lake Sam Rayburn on a cloudy and misty February day. We decided to head to the back end of a creek to some flats in five feet of water. We were hoping to catch some bass coming up out of the creek and moving onto the flats. We chose to throw crawfish-colored, lipless crank baits on the edges of the creek and catch some of the fish moving up. The two of us started catching good fish right away just by moving up and down the creek for about three hundred yards, fishing the edges. We just happened to hit the area at the right time and literally caught good fish all day long. The trip was one for the books, a time when all the pieces fall into place. The weather along with the water conditions worked together to give us one of those memorable days on the lake. As we slowly worked our lures along the bottom, we were repeatedly greeted with the hard thump of an aggressive bass. We spent an entire day catching bass from three to seven pounds, without ever having to wait long for a strike. We boated well over a hundred bass that day, with the majority of them fish being four to five pounds. Those types of days don't come around too often, but if you understand the movements of the bass at different times of the year, you have a chance of putting yourself in line for a day like that sooner or later.

Take the time to visualize the creek channels as they wander through the area, and try to find those sweet spots where the creeks run up against a point, or where the channel cuts in close to the shoreline. Many times that productive shallow water spot you like will have a creek channel nearby, making the area very appealing to the wary mature fish. The creek channel is the travel route that is bringing the fish into that area. Remember the bends in the creek channels and junctions in your search for schooling bass; they are the areas along the creek that give the fish more options in their feeding while giving you more options in intercepting those fish. The fish use these bends and junctions to give them more area of ambush so they can adjust their attacking point as the bait changes its patterns. Try to get to a point where you almost know the lay of the whole cove as if it contained no water at all; in other words, know it like the back of your hand.

There are some very under-fished honey holes that you can find along the creek channels in the areas you fish. One of the main keys to these spots is the type of cover that is available to the fish to ambush prey and feel safe. The creek itself is a great form of structure, and when you can find cover on that structure for the fish to use as an ambush point, all the better. If you are someone who likes to set up his own cover in the form of brush piles, creek intersections and creek bends are hard to beat, and if the laws in the lake you fish allow, these manmade honey holes can draw bass for many years. As the brush pile starts to age, you can keep it the bass haven you want by adding a bag of cattle range cubes from time to time to keep the bait happy. As you map the creek channel you like, the way the bait positions itself at a certain location will help you decide on the depths to key on when looking for, or adding, cover. All of this requires spending the time to know the area you fish.

As spring turns to summer, the fish will make a much more scattered journey back to the river channel, gorging themselves on bait fish as they go, many times spending time on the nearby flats running the edges of the grass, feeding on the available bait. When summer arrives, the fish will set up on their very predictable summer haunts in the depths of the river channel. It is at this time that the fish are more predictable in their feeding than they are all year long. At the end of the summer, the fish will make a good push back up the creeks to take advantage of the shad migration. This is a yearly thing, and a lot of fishermen don't take advantage of the move quickly enough to enjoy the bounty it brings. In late August, the bass will start to move very shallow chasing these shad. Many times they go unmolested because the heat of the summer still lingers, and many fishermen think the bass won't enter that warm water. This time of year has long been a favorite time of mine to catch some real good fish in very shallow water. They will attack the shad with abandon, behaving quite reckless at times. The key is to mimic the shad they feed on. Nowadays, I don't fish a spinner bait in shallow water as much as I did when I was a kid, but I do like this time of year to relive those old days. The bait I have the most success with at this time of year is the black and white, single spin H&H spinner bait. This little spinner bait produces the vibration that I have a lot of confidence in, and the black and white color resembles a shad closely enough. I like this bait in shallow and deep water, as well as for a very productive night time lure. Don't forget about this tried and true favorite. Whichever lure you choose, just make sure that it closely resembles a shad, which is the prey the bass are targeting at this time of year.

Get to know the ins and outs of the creek channels in your part of the lake. These bass highways are there waiting for you to tap into some of the best fishing on your lake. The effort you spend will surely be rewarded by the numbers of good bass you start to catch. When targeting these channels, you are putting yourself right in the travel routes the fish use, and because of that, you are setting the stage to meet the bass on its own terms. Once you know the area as if it were void of water, move to the next creek, and with hard work, you can double your pleasure.

Humps and Ridges

These types of structures are the true gems of the deep water fisherman. Humps and ridges have schools of bass that move on and off of these sweet spots throughout the day and night. Above all else, you need to take the time to find these spots on the lake you fish; the effort can put some incredible bass fishing in your reach. Humps are more or less hilltops under the water level, and ridges are just longer rifts running on for a little distance. Both are similar rises off the bottom, and both seem to have a great ability to draw in bait and the opportunistic bass.

There is not a visible sign on the shoreline to show you their presence, or anything to give you a clue to their location like you have when finding creeks or points, but their hidden bounty is worth any amount of time spent locating them. The way to find these hidden areas, besides using maps, which will put you on some good community holes, is to get out in the boat and run. While running, keep an eye on your electronics for any depth change you encounter. When you see a depth change, immediately turn around and cover the area completely, until the bottom contour for that area is visible in your mind. You are looking for structure that drops off on all sides, and it will usually take going back and forth over these areas several times to see this. You may have to repeat this many times until that special magic spot is found, but it is well worth it. Also, locating other unexpected changes in the bottom structure can many times yield a productive surprise. Finding a good change in the bottom makeup, or discovering a hidden brush pile or submerged standing timber can make the search for these hidden gems worthwhile. Don't give up; these spots are out there somewhere. Just keep on searching until you really can't search anymore. Once you locate a hump or ridge, cover the entire area with your electronics to get an idea of the complete makeup of the structure. Make special note of any cover on the structure; sometimes these areas will be only a small rise off the bottom on your graph. A small piece of brush or a small rock pile could be the main attractor on the entire structure, so don't cover it too quickly, or you might miss the spot of a lifetime. There is a good chance you will see fish and bait on your electronics over these areas, but now is not the time to fish. Get to know the structure you have found, and save the fishing for another time. Learn to fight the urge to react on visible fish and to spend more time searching.

You will have to get an idea of the area surrounding a hump or ridge to see where the sweet spots will be. You will have to find the travel routes and signposts the fish are using to move onto the structure. Humps and ridges usually will have a sloping side and most often will have a side that is a little steeper. The fish will usually prefer the steepest area to move in and out on, but get to know the whole area so you don't miss good fish holding cover. Locate any channels or timber that are around the structure, or maybe even be an intersecting ridge or trough. Something around the structure is going to be the key to moving schools of bass into the area. As you graph the structure, you will notice whether the area has a good supply of forage. If a lot of bait is available, you know there is a travel route for fish to follow to the structure.

River channels, creek channels, points, humps, and ridges are all good places to start when looking for schools of quality bass. The time spent in search of these locations can pay off big. I hope this information will get you away from the shorelines you depend on and get you out into deeper water, so you can start to understand the true habits of schooling bass. Later in the book we will discuss the way to find those productive shorelines, but for now you have to get a grasp on the movements of the school-oriented bass and start to increase the number of fish you put in your boat.

Go over in your mind the plan of action you are going to implement on your lake to find the sweet spots in your area. No matter how tough it seems, stay with that plan until you succeed in finding at least one good offshore spot to fish. This will start to make a huge difference in the amount of confidence you have on your lake, and that confidence will lead you to find more spots like that one while also raising the overall size of the fish you catch. I hope leading with this information will get you started right away in changing your mindset while out fishing—to the mindset of looking deep.

To recap, find underwater structure at or close to the thermocline depth. This depth, especially during the summer, supplies the best oxygen range for the bass that, along with the water temperature, gives the bass a very comfortable zone in which to live. The thermocline is more pronounced in the summer months, usually starting a little shallower in the early part of the year and descending as the heat grows. This area will remain productive until the cooling nights of the fall cause the cooler surface water to actually sink past the warmer water below, a lake turnover if you will. This is a time when the bass prefer not to be in deep water, wanting to take advantage of the cooler temperatures. Remember to look for the cover on the deep water structure to find that mother lode of quality fish. And the fish will move shallow before the fall to follow the shad and avoid the lake's turnover. Even if you feel you should fish the shallows as the sun comes up, fight that feeling because that is also the best time to be fishing the deeper structure.

Establishing a Pattern

Establishing a pattern for the day's fishing is the one thing that can make or break the day on the lake. If you decide just to fish your way to the fish, along a good-looking shoreline where you might have caught a few fish in the past, for instance, your arm is going fall off before you ever have a chance to come up with a good fishable pattern. That shoreline might have hundreds of great-looking spots to cast to, but in all honesty, only about ten percent of the targets, at most, will hold fish, and most of the time these fish won't be the quality you should be looking for. If you want to start on a shoreline, take the weather and water conditions into consideration and begin in a shallow area that has a previously located travel route from deep water leading to it. A simple start on a fishy looking shoreline is doomed to failure.

Start each day you go fishing by looking at the weather and water conditions, along with the time of year. After processing the conditions, decide where the best place to start that day will be. You have to visualize what the fish are doing at that time and begin in a place you feel will put the most fish within reach to establish a pattern. Have confidence that the place you choose to start will pay off right off the bat. Confidence is the key to succeeding when trying to establish a pattern. Once you catch four or five quality fish from a certain area, you have found a pattern. Try to repeat this tactic in similar locations, and you should have a good start already on the day's outcome. Remember to visualize what the fish are doing and make them work for you. As soon as you feel a pattern is slowing down in one area, quickly move to a new spot to reestablish a pattern for the new conditions.

In the late eighties, my wife and I were having our yard landscaped at our home on Lake Conroe. It was late August, and the first strong front of the year was going to move through in a few hours. As I looked out on the lake, I could actually visualize in my mind the bass going crazy on the shad at a certain location. I informed my wife I just had to go fishing and definitely would be back in a couple of hours. I motored my boat to a drop-off that intersected a creek channel at a 90-degree angle just off of the Del Lago Resort. I killed my big engine and used the trolling motor to hit the place where the top of the drop-off hit the channel and threw out a marker buoy. The first thing I noticed when I turned around to fish was that the surface was littered with stunned and dying shad; this told me the activity below the surface was indeed as I had visualized it. I knew I had made a good choice in putting off my duties at the house. I put on a half-ounce spoon and cast to the deep water of the creek. After letting the spoon sink, I started to bounce the spoon up the drop-off and was immediately rewarded with a solid thump, and a five pound bass came to the surface, confirming what I had thought. I put the bass in the boat, released it, and sent my spoon back into the depths again, repeating the bouncing action up the drop-off. The action was great, and for the next two hours I put about thirty to forty bass between three and seven pounds in the boat, along with about twenty white bass, a dozen or so crappie, and a few big hybrid stripers to top it off. After my first-front-of-the-year itch was scratched, I picked up my marker buoy and headed to the house completely satisfied. The weather conditions we had that day led me to visualize a scenario playing out on the lake, and my confidence rewarded me with two hours of great fishing. Take into consideration the weather and water conditions, along with the time of year, and start a great day of fishing even before you hit the water. By making a plan in advance, you can eliminate any indecision you might have when you're out on the lake.

It is important to build the plan of the day in your mind before launching your boat on the lake. By taking into consideration the time of year as well as the water and wind conditions, you have started to win the battle before it even starts. All of this will play a strong role in the way you approach a day on the lake in the future. This will lead you to start using the most valuable tool you have, your mind. You will have to come up with an idea of what the fishes' behavior will be for the conditions at hand and create a plan of attack. You will have to decide which lures will work best for the present conditions, as well as where to start your search, in order to have the most success.

The cover you will have to choose from when starting the day can be daunting at times. Do I start on the points or a creek channel or maybe on the shoreline cover? Will the fish be in the grass or on a grass line? Maybe a drop-off next to the flats will pay off, or maybe the flats themselves will be the key to finding active fish. All of these things are going to play out in your mind as you come up with a plan. Another thing to put into your mental computer is the lake level. Is the lake level falling at this time, or is the lake on the rise? This little factor can affect a fish's behavior about as much as anything you will encounter. It might be one of the main things you process first when deciding on a starting point for that morning. When the lake is on the rise, the fish will push back into the hard to reach areas on the shorelines and in the back of creeks, taking advantage of newly accessible forage. The fish will spread out and cover the hard to reach shallows, attacking the bait fish and other prey that are moving into the area to forage on the small morsels the high water has brought them. The shallowest of flats in the back areas that have creeks coming into them can be a great place to venture into; you can take advantage of the fish that are setting up on the ambush points the current has created. Always try to take advantage of the currents available in the creeks when the water is on the rise. These will always be spots where the bass will try to set up on, catching the bait that washes down with the current.

Youngest son Grant with his best bass

When the lake is falling, the bass can seem to be a little harder to catch and can sometimes seem almost impossible to locate. If you know the surrounding area that you are fishing, finding these fish can be as easy as one, two, three. First, you have to get an idea of how fast the lake is falling. The water marks on the shoreline cover can sometimes give this away. If the lake is on a slow fall, the fish well set up on the first line of structure or cover from the shallows. Maybe the fish will set up on the outside edge of the brush they had been holding on, or maybe on the inside or outside edge of a grass line off that same brush. Second, if the lake is falling quite rapidly, the first place to start would be the outside edge of the grass line; then try out to the first drop-off or creek channel. The faster the water level falls, the farther away from the shallows the fish will prefer. Many times the fish don't want to deal with relocating and, depending on the rate of drop, will move to an area that they feel will be a place they can stay. The rate at which the lake falls is very important to finding where the bass will set up. A lake level, whether it is constant, rising, or falling, is a good place to start when patterning fish for that day.

The next area to explore in uncovering the fishes' behavior for a certain day is the clarity of the water. My rule of thumb is that the clearer the water, the deeper I fish. If shallow water is the plan of the day, I usually consider four to six feet to be shallow in clear water. For the deep water, you can venture out into water as deep as forty feet and still find fish. Fish feel safe in the deep water of clear lakes.

In stained water, the shallows might be in the two- to four-foot range, with the deep water being in the ten- to twelve-foot range. Fish will seem to be a little more active in the shallows when the water is a bit stained. They feel safer and most of the time won't burrow as far back into the cover as in clear water, and the direction of the sunlight isn't as important when setting up on ambush points. Your approach to these fish doesn't have to be as stealthy as in clear water either, but still be mindful of the noise and your silhouette. Fish can still see for a good ways in stained water; this will give you a few more choices of lures to use. Pitching and flipping can be done at a little faster pace, and a lot more water can be covered when a faster pace is used. Once you get a feel for where the fish are setting up on the cover, you can slow down and pick the area apart.

Now in muddy or off-colored water, which has always been my favorite, I usually define the shallow water as from about six inches out to the deep water, which I consider to be six feet or so. If I am going to flip or pitch when I'm on the water, I am going to look for off-colored water. This water might be up the river or on a windblown point. Wherever the water is the muddiest is where I want to start. You will be surprised how far a fish can see in muddy water. The spots I like the best are bushes that line the shore between the main point and the secondary point and that have plenty of wind blowing in on them. Usually I like very off-colored water with foam and trash on the surface; these seem to be the areas where

I catch good numbers of big fish while flipping. In this case, I will throw a black and blue jig with a bulky black trailer. One other thing is that I always use a rattle on my jigs. The subtle clicks of the rattle seem to entice more fish to hit the bait.

The key to fishing off-colored water is the vibration of the bait, along with a dark color. When I was about fifteen years old, my father invited me to a friend's lake just south of Houston to enjoy some bass fishing. This lake has produced many good fish over the years and was a favorite of ours. The way we always fished the lake was to take a boat to the good areas, then wade fish the area. This was always exciting, especially because of the number of alligators in the lake. When we arrived we found the lake very low, and extremely muddy. The plan was to swim across the canals that bordered the edges of the lake and wade along the grass line, casting on the edge of the canal. The bait I decided on was a black Pico Perch crank bait that had three holes drilled through the center. My father went with a dark green, and the gentleman who owned the lake chose a spinner bait. They let me off at a spot along the levee and then they headed off to fish another part of the lake. I swam across the canal and started wading the grass line. On my second cast I hooked a monster fish that cleared the water and threw my bait. I was sick; it was surely the biggest fish I had ever hooked. On the next cast, my offering was inhaled by a nice seven-pound bass, and because the owner was letting the lake fall so he could kill the fish population and restock it, I strung the fish. The owner would kill the fish population about every twelve years or so to clear out the trash fish that the birds constantly brought into the lake. After a cast or two, my bait was stopped by another big fish which, after a great fight, I placed on the stringer with the other fish. The memory of losing that first fish quickly faded as I put big fish after big fish on my stringer. I covered about a mile or so and had caught big fish the whole time. The stringer I was hauling became impossible to move, so I decided to call it a day, and what a day it was. I pushed the stringer out into the canal and swam to the other side and staked the fish out. There was no way I could lift the haul and would hate to let an alligator get them, so I ran back to the house to get help.

As I came up to the house, the other two fishermen were relaxing with a drink on the deck. I told them that I needed help with my fish because I couldn't lift the stringer. They laughed, not believing me, showing me that my father had only caught one fish and that Robbie had only caught four on the spinner bait. After a little begging I convinced them to bring the car and help me load the fish. After driving to the spot where I had left the fish, they were shocked when they walked through the reeds and saw that massive stringer of fish floating in the water. It took all of us to load the fish and unload them at the house. It was the best day I had ever had in bass fishing up to that point. The stringer had twenty-three bass on it, and we weighed the largest and the smallest. The smallest was about four pounds, ten ounces, and the biggest was eight pounds, two ounces. It was an incredible stringer to gaze on, and that was a day I will always remember. At that time in my life I considered these fish to be huge, and I guess they were. But this was my first experience with numbers of good fish, and it set the goal high for me the rest of my fishing days; since then I have always worked hard at staying at that level. The key to this amazing catch of big fish was the bait I used in that muddy water. The black bait, along with the vibration created by the holes drilled into it, is what attracted the fish to the lure. Always keep that in mind when fishing off-colored water, and never shy away from water you feel is too muddy to catch fish in.

When trying to coax bass to hit in shallow water in clearer conditions, I will use a more natural color to my jig or soft plastic, and will downsize the bulk of the bait to increase the fall rate. I don't want the fish to have a good look at the bait; I want them to react on it instead. Another thing I always do in clear or off-colored water when fishing shallow water: if it starts to rain I will immediately pick up a spinner bait and work the same cover inside and out. I don't know what it is about the rain turning on the fish to a spinner bait, but it works. I can't say how many times I have done this with good results. Next time it starts to rain, try this and I think you will be surprised.

Remember, when you choose the shallow area you wish to fish, make sure you have done your homework and discovered what is bringing the fish to that area. Maybe it is a creek channel that cuts in close to the shore, or maybe a stump row leading the fish in from deeper water. Whatever it is, just make sure there is a travel route leading the fish to your area. This will give you the confidence you need to make the fish literally do what you want them to do. Don't laugh—it's true. There are plenty of resident fish living on most of an entire lake, although most of these fish are young. But to catch the quality fish you want, the bigger school fish, you will have to entice them into the area you are fishing. They will have to have a defined travel route in and out of the area.

Get off the beaten path! The fun you can have while venturing off the beaten path can give you some of the greatest memories you will ever have in your bass fishing experiences. I can't count how many times I made the effort to deviate from the norm and was rewarded with some great bass fishing. Years back on Lake Conroe, when I didn't have a guide party, I would move back into a few of my favorite creeks as far as I could get my boat. It would be spring, so I knew there were some big, unmolested bass waiting to be caught for the angler who was willing to leave the boat and wade in on these fish. This was a technique I used many times on lakes like Gibbons Creek and Sam Rayburn, and I have been blessed with some great memories from doing so. I usually targeted these fish with plastic lizards, as most fish were on the bed. Many times I got the fish to hit on maybe the twentieth cast. You had to spend time with these fish, but the big females were worth the time spent. A lot of times I would work a floating lizard over the fishes' nest time after time until I felt the fish was ready; then I would swap out with a sinking lizard and drop the bait right on the nest, and the fish would go crazy. Many times it's the little changes in tactics that will trigger fish to hit when they aren't in the mood.

I remember times on Sam Rayburn in the summer, moving to the back reaches of small creeks to the thick willows. My brother-in-law Gary and I would painstakingly drag the boat with our hands back through the willows and target fish, with floating lizards, that have never been fished for. The overall size of some of these bass was amazing at times, and then horsing them out of the cover was sometimes sheer hand-to-hand combat, but it was well worth it. I love doing these types of things to broaden my fishing adventures. Don't be afraid to try something different or to think out of the box; the rewards can be great, and the memories special.

To establish a pattern on fish when you just know that the fish are in the area can be a little tricky at times. When you feel you have chosen an area that should be holding fish, this is a good time to try to get them to reveal themselves. A crank bait or a spinner bait is a good choice is this endeavor. In my later years I have gotten a little lazy at times, so I will hit a good area and let a search bait do my work and clue me in to what the fish are doing. You don't always have to get a hit to find fish. Just pay attention to any followers that might give away their presence.

On Canyon Lake near my home, I use this tactic a lot in the clear water that dominates the lake. I will hit a high confidence area on the upper third of the lake, throwing a rattletrap that resembles shad or crawfish. The key to this is to watch the bait as it nears the boat. Many times if you don't catch a fish, you will see a fish follow the lure and then turn away. Lures are tools, so I use them as tools to locate fish. When I finally see this, I will slow down and fish the area with jigs and soft plastics and will usually catch plenty of hefty fish. Anything you can use to help you pattern fish is a tool, so you should use the tools you have in your arsenal to help you narrow down the fishes' behavior at that time.

Many times you can cover a creek channel edge with a deep diving crank bait to locate the spots where the bass are holding on in that area, then slow down and pick the area apart with a more finesse type bait until it's time to move on and find the next school of bass. Usually when you do find the fish, they will be set up on a certain type of feature on that creek channel, a feature you might not have even known was there. When you don't know exactly how the fish are using a certain area, using a search bait will eliminate wasted time spent searching with a slow moving lure.

Another tactic to help locate fish in shallow water is to look for the fish-eating water birds grouped in an area. This will always indicate the presence of bait fish, which will also lead you to the bass. Many times when you look you will actually see minnows or shad skipping in the shallows, and this is a good indicator that predators are probably in the area. Always look for any sign you can to help alert you to the presence of catchable bass. If bass don't show themselves after a short time at any location, don't spend time trying to make something happen. Move to a new location and start the search anew. When you are only catching juvenile fish in a certain spot, it is also time to move. Don't waste time on small fish. When fish are known to be in an area and holding on a certain cover, don't be afraid of making multiple casts in order to entice a dormant fish to hit. At times it might take ten to fifteen casts to get these fish to hit, but you have to know the fish are there, or there is no way to spend that much time on a fish without going crazy. Fish can be coerced into hitting a bait, so when you know the fish are there try to spend at least a little time trying to make them hit.

One quick way to look for a pattern is to key on the places where two different types of cover meet. This tactic has always been a good one and has work for me in the past. I don't know what it is about the intersection of two different covers that attracts the fish, but the spot where the two covers meet is worth a look. It might be a lay down log in some thick grass, or maybe where the heavy grass meets a rock pile. Whatever it is, jumping around an area that is holding fish and targeting only these types of spots might reveal a pattern without your wasting much time. When you catch a good fish in a certain location or in a certain form of cover, make note of everything that was involved in the catching of that fish and see if it can be duplicated in a similar type area; this could lead you to uncover a pattern. You have to notice when a pattern reveals itself to you in order to be able to take advantage of it, so pay attention to every little detail that involved in when and where fish are caught. Always try thinking of ways to eliminate wasted time on the water, and noticing a pattern quickly is a good place to start.

Catching the Big Girls

When patterning the upper end bass in the lake you fish, fish over the size of the usual three to five pounders, it will take a little different approach to put one of these fish on the end of your line. These bass are much older and a lot more wary than the more common immature fish usually encountered, and they have learned what it takes to keep safe while feeding. These fish are a lot more definite in the way they move about and are more precise in the places they choose to set up on to feed and to sit dormant. Big fish don't feed nearly as often as smaller fish and will feed on much larger prey so they can stay in safe locations for longer periods at a time and thus avoid spending time chasing smaller bait around. The most consistent way to find the upper end fish is to spend the necessary time finding their deep water haunts. These fish will find small defined areas on a river or creek channels and set up camp. One of these sweet spots might be a small ledge that gives the fish access to a lot of food as well as access to deep water for safety, or that gives her an easy move to the shallows when the urge strikes. The key is finding the spots in the depths that have it all. The big fish has earned the best spots to hold on, so learn to notice the little hints these areas can offer. You have to spend a lot of time in these deep water areas with your electronics to find the sweet spots. It is worth any amount of time you spend because when you come across one of these deep water haunts you can pull big fish off of the spot for years to come.

For those who want to spend a lot less time searching the depths than the many hours it takes to find the big fish, the next best thing is to catch these fish as they move shallow to reproduce. Big bass know from experience what the season brings and are usually some of the first fish to make their move to the shallows at the first hint of the spring's warming trend. They will quickly move up the creeks, knowing exactly where they want to be from their many years of making that same trip. Because of this quick, deliberate movement, many times they are hard to intercept on the creek channel hangouts like the younger fish, so knowing where they prefer to set up will help you encounter one of these giants. The upper end bass will set up on the back of a creek that gives them an ambush point and easy access to food, along with an easy move to deep water in the case of danger or adverse weather. If the lake you fish is void of weeds, look for these fish at an average depth of about ten feet, right next to a creek channel. The fish will set up in the heaviest brush or cover they can find. If your lake is blessed with thick weeds such as hydrilla, your search will be a little easier. The big fish will set up house in a thick mat of hydrilla. In early spring, the main deterrents to a fish's comfort are cloud cover and wind. The bass will use the weeds to dampen any wave action and then let the sun's rays warm them as they sit and wait to make the move shallow when the weather warms. Although cloud cover can aid you most of the year by pulling fish out of the cover, while helping them in their search for food without the sun hampering their vision, the cloud cover in the early spring will send the fish back to the depths of the weeds to find a more comfortable zone. When wind is added to the equation, fish will look for a more stable area to be.

Big bass have seen everything nature has to offer, and over the years they have found ways to avoid the bouts of wind and clouds. To take advantage of this on a weed-filled lake, look for the heaviest mat of weeds next to the nearest creek channel. The big bass will set up in these weeds for definite reasons. First, they have access to deep water if the weather does get too rough for comfort. Second, they have a controlled travel route for the bait to move right into their attack area. The next key is that the fish can move up and down as needed in the mat to create the environment they want. When the weather stabilizes after a front, the fish will set up high in the mat and soak in the sun. The mat will block all wind, and the water will be a few degrees warmer than the surrounding water. Just a few degrees in temperature will mean a lot to a bass. When a front moves through, the fish can settle deep in the grass and wait out the adverse conditions until the sun makes another appearance. A few things to remember: You need to find bait in the weeds you choose to search. You also need to make a note of how close shallow water breeding areas are to the weed mat. An easy deep water access route, along with a quick and easy travel route to the spawning area, are things that are important to the older fish. Remember, the wind is not your friend in cold water. The fish will move deep in the cover or move to the deeper edges to feed when the wind and clouds make it a little too uncomfortable for their liking. As the water starts to warm as the spring progresses, the wind and cloud cover will not be a deterrent at that point. The places where the big fish set up on to make their move shallow are going to be the places you want to try to catch them. These fish are going to move into an area that makes it hard for anyone to get to them while they reproduce, so catching them at that point can seem almost impossible.

As the water temperature starts to move into the sixties, the fish will make a migration to the shallows. This does not mean the fish will always have a successful spawn; there are many things that can deter this reproduction process. The fish will spawn on the full moons of March, April, and May, depending on the weather. When the fish move up to spawn and a hard cold front hits, the fish will move off to deeper water and wait out the cooling trend. Many times these fish will not move back up until the next full moon cycle. Weather can really affect a spawning season more than people think, and sometimes can hurt it so severely that there will be a huge decrease in the amount of fish in that year's class. When a good spawning area is located, this area will draw the attention of a lot of fish, so always recheck the area for a new batch of egg-laden fish. The area will draw groups of bass staging up to make their move shallow, so find the structure or cover they are staging on and try to intercept the bass there. Remember the big fish don't feed as often as the smaller fish do, so you will have to keep checking the high percentage spots until you encounter one of the big females.

Another good time to intercept the big females is when they move off of the nests and stage up on the first line of cover to gorge themselves to replenish their bodies. These fish know from experience where the best food is going to be and the type of food that will replenish their bodies the fastest after the rigors of spawning. As the water warms and the choices in foods go up, these fish will stay in the shallows to take advantage of the new offerings. Crawfish, frogs, and other critters start to emerge after the long winter. The big fish in the area will lower their cautious nature at this time while they build up their bodies drained by the spawn. This is the best time of year to throw red or bright green baits. These colors, especially the red baits, seem to trigger the reflex action of the bass. One thing you can do to boost your odds is to visit the good spots a few times a day to try to intercept one of these big girls because they will be feeding at some point in the day or night. This is the time of year when I will almost exclusively stay with the crawfish colors. I find that the size of the bass I catch is a little better on these baits. Bass know that the crawfish in the area will give their bodies what they need more than most other forms of prey, so they will always try to feed on crawfish when they can. Therefore, it's a great time of year to put an imitation in front of them.

One often overlooked tactic for catching a trophy fish is to venture out on the water after dark. The nights before and after the full moon can put heavy fish in an accessible location for the adventurous fisherman. When you can find stable weather conditions after a front that coincides with the full moon, it is worth the effort to have the lake to yourself in the pursuit of that lunker of a lifetime. These fish will move up into shallower water that they would never feel comfortable enough to enter in daylight hours. And these fish will be extremely spooky, so you need to take as much care as you can not to alert them to your presence. The most consistent way to catch good fish at night is to fish the same deeper structure you fish during the day. The fish will move onto these areas to feed at night, and the key is to be there when they do. There are times when the action is very good, and in no time at all you can get your fill of good fishing on one of these nights. On most nights the fishing can be a little slow, so you will have to have a lot of patience to wait for the fish to feed. The key is to be on a good area of structure such as a point or ridge, and sit there as long as it takes to catch a big fish. Try not to let the boredom get to you and make you move prematurely. If you are in a good area you trust, try to wait the fish out; this is a great way to catch a monster fish that is very hard to catch during the day.

If your goal is to catch that bass of a lifetime, you will find no other time of the year when these fish will be so accessible as during the spawn. The spawn will put fish at your finger tips that at all other times are set up in their hard-to-reach habitat. When the big females are through with the reproduction cycle and replenish their bodies, they will quickly migrate down the creeks and get back to their little sweet spots as soon as they can so that they feel safe and secure. So when this happens, get on the lake with your electronics and open the window wider for your search for that fish of your dreams. Try to fish for these big fish at night when you get the chance. It is a very peaceful way to fish, and you will have no traffic at all to contend with. It's worth a sleepless night to catch a fish of a lifetime.

When targeting big bass, you have to be firm in your convictions that you are searching for that fish of a lifetime in the proper location. Any doubt will surely hamper you in reaching your intended goal. Get to know the habits of the top end fish in your area, and stay focused on the search area you wish to concentrate on. Always remember that these heavy weights have encountered many fishermen throughout their life in that lake, and you must think out of the box to be able to trick wary fish into biting. Many times when the larger fish are the target, many hours can pass without a hit, so stay vigilant in your pursuit, keep your confidence at a high level, and you will more than likely achieve your goal.

A real heavy weight

Confidence is the Key

There is no other factor in bass fishing that is so important to the success of your fishing than confidence. Many anglers say how important confidence is, but they never explain what they mean by confidence. In my Fishing Magic book about the Texas coast, I really go into the importance of mindset while fishing. You have to create the success you want to have in your mind before you go out on the lake and catch the numbers of quality fish you desire. The Law of Attraction is an extremely strong asset you have while fishing; it is something you need to learn how to harness before you ever put your boat in the lake. If you find yourself in a negative state of mind, and you don't think the fish are going to bite, guess what— they won't! You have got to visualize the fish doing what you want them to do and moving in on your lure, and definitely visualize the strike. This might sound a little out there, but it is the most important thing I have learned in my many years of fishing, and it is the one thing to which I can attribute the great success I have had since I was a kid. It is a true fact of nature for all of us and can play a big part in our lives if we use it for all it's worth. Try to learn techniques that will enable you to stay in a positive state of mind.

When you find yourself starting to get into a negative frame of mind, learn to turn your mind back to the positive. Find some mental visual aids to put you back into a positive frame of mind, and then find ways to stay in that mindset. Maybe envision a fish moving in for a strike on your lure as you work it back to the boat, and really feel it. Whatever it is, this ability is going to be the greatest tool you have the rest of your life while out fishing. A trick I use many times when I am not quite in the moment is to visualize a fishing spot or some structure that is going to turn my day around if I hit that spot right now, and then I will move to that spot to find the success I know is waiting. Guess what—it works!

A few years ago, I was fishing on Lake Sam Rayburn with my brother-in-law Gary. It was late May, and we hadn't quite put together a good pattern we could rely on. I told Gary we needed to make a change and try something a little different. I informed him we definitely needed to move to an area with some pepper grass, because at this time of year I have always had a great deal of success fishing pepper grass with lightly weighted worms. To my surprise, Gary informed me that he hated to fish pepper grass and had never had any success in doing so. He let me know in no uncertain terms that he had no confidence in such a move and tried to change my mind. I wasn't going to let that comment deter me from the path I set of changing my frame of mind, so I urged him to make the move. He unhappily said there was a large area of pepper grass on the north side of Bird Island that came all the way up close to the brush, so he headed off to prove to me that you don't catch fish in pepper grass. We set up off a little point of brush right in the middle of his detested pepper grass and started to probe the vegetation. I knew that I could prove him wrong, and guess what—things were a little different than Gary expected them to be, and I think now that he was probably very happy they were. On Gary's first four casts into the "unproductive" grass, he happened to put four hefty three- to four-pound bass in the boat. I was really enjoying the idea that you supposedly couldn't catch fish in pepper grass when Gary set the hook on his fifth fish. The beautiful fish made a pass right by the back of the boat, giving me a great look at her size. I casually looked up and informed Gary that he had the best fish he had ever caught on the end of his line. He shot back, "Don't tell me that," and proceeded to bring the fish to the boat. After it came to the boat, I reached down and lipped the big fish and just couldn't help myself—I acted as if I had just dropped her back into the lake. Seeing the look on Gary's face, I quickly decided to bring the fish into the boat for my own safety. The bass weighed 12 pounds and was the biggest bass he had ever caught. After the high fives and taking a few pictures, I looked at Gary and said, "Pepper grass, huh?" Now every time we fish together, I ask him what he thinks about fishing pepper grass, and his answer is always the same. He says he loves fishing pepper grass, he has always loved fishing pepper grass, and it is probably his favorite type of cover to fish.

Gary's 12-pound Pepper Grass Bass

I can't stress enough how important your mindset is when it comes to taking your fishing to the next level. It is easy to write this off as another wild, harebrained system of catching fish, but trust me: this positive mindset is really a vital part of fishing when you want to become the type of angler that you always hoped to be. Think back on some of the days you had good success while on the water; think about the mindset you had. More than likely you were in a positive state of mind when you started catching fish, and you probably didn't even have the time to become negative. Think about some of the bad days you've had on the lake. Try to remember if the day started off slow and if you let yourself start to think that the fish weren't going to bite no matter what you did. More than likely you decided the fishing would be tough, and guess what, that day did materialize into a tough one because you projected that in your mind. I know, it sounds crazy, but I strongly feel it is a very real phenomenon, and you should pay more attention to your frame of mind when fishing.

You have to find ways to keep a positive frame of mind. Maybe coming up with a fish-catching scene you can play in your mind will help you outwit the bad thoughts until you can push back that negativity that is humming in your brain. Visualize this scene over and over in your head, and maybe add a positive transition in your mind to how that mental fish catching will actually start to play out in day you are having. What the mind can do for you should not be brushed aside; this is the most powerful fish-catching tool you have at your disposal. You need to learn how to control the workings of your mind when you're on the water and make your mind work for you in every part of your fishing day.

In my book on fishing the Texas coast I talked about keeping a log of your fishing trips. This is not a log about how the fishing trip went, but instead a log of how the trip will go. What I mean by this is to make a log, or plan if you will, of how the trip is going to be. Make your plans for the trip, taking into account the time of year and the weather and water conditions; decide where you will go and plan the success you will have at these locations. You will be surprised later when you look back at the log to see how it played a strong part in the day you had.

That's about as far as I will go for now into the aspect of making your mind a big part of your fishing; I just want you to realize the unbelievable magic your mind can create in the success of your fishing. Remember, the mind is a terrible thing to waste.

Spinner Baits

The great thing about spinner baits is that they are easy to fish, and almost anyone who can cast a rod can use them and catch fish. This being said, there are many different presentations you can use with this bait to increase your productivity for certain situations.

The type of spinner bait we will cover in this section is the open safety pin type, a v-shaped wire harness with a single or double spinner blade on one side and a lead head holding the hook on the other. Although there are spinner baits on the market with more than two spinner blades, we will cover the single and double blade versions. These baits can be used throughout every month of the year with good success, and they have a knack for producing some really big fish. The spinner bait doesn't seem to resemble anything in nature, so I suspect the fish attack the bait because they haven't ever seen anything so ugly, and they don't want it cross-breeding with their young. But seriously, I feel the bait attracts the fish by flash and vibration.

The most popular sizes for these baits are the 3/16-oz., 1/4-oz. and the 1/2-oz. models, referring to the weight of the head. I will usually stay with these sizes for all applications. When I do fish the bait in very deep water, sometimes as deep as thirty feet, I will use a 1/4-oz. or larger, rubber core sinker with the rubber removed and crimp the weight on the wire ahead of the spinner bait's head, or crimp it to the upper part of the hook shank below the head. When it comes to the blades, I will choose them depending on the circumstances in which I am fishing. When I am fishing the lure in a fashion to attract schooling fish or I am burning the bait on the top, I prefer the softer vibration of two blades. When burning the bait at the surface, I prefer twin Colorado blades with a weight added to the bait to keep it below the surface of the water. The blades create lift, and the added weight will help keep the lure below the surface. When I am throwing a spinner bait lure at schooling fish, I will use twin willow leaf blades and a skirt color closely matching the bait the fish are feeding on. The willow blades have a little less vibration than the Colorado blades, so I depend more on the flash of the bait, with the soft vibration drawing fish to hit. No matter what the circumstances are when I'm fishing the spinner bait, I will impart some type of action to the bait. Sometimes I will add a little hop to the the lure by popping my rod tip, and sometimes I will give the bait a pause in the retrieve. I feel it's important to add a little change to the retrieve of the bait to entice a strike from a following fish.

When fishing off-colored or deep water or when fishing at night, I will use a single Colorado blade. This presentation gives off an incredible amount of vibration, and with a large blade you can feel the thumps of the blade all the way up your arm with each turn of the reel handle. In deep water I will add a weight to a single-bladed bait and keep the bait in contact with the bottom. The two retrieves I will normally use are a slow rolling technique and a bottom hopping technique. To slow roll the bait, I will cast the bait out and pull a little extra line off the reel to allow the bait to fall at the end of the cast instead of falling toward the boat. When the bait hits the bottom I will start a slow crawl of the bait back to the boat, pausing every few turns of the handle to make sure the bait stays in close contact with the bottom. The strikes are easy to detect; the fish will usually hammer the lure, leaving no doubt you have had a hit. At night or in shallower applications I will do the same thing, but without the added weight. The bottom bouncing technique is one of my favorite in mid-level to deep water or at night. I will not add any extra weight to the single blade bait when using this technique. I will cast the bait out and let it settle on the bottom, and then on a tight line I will pick up the bait about a foot or so off the bottom, making sure I can feel the vibration of the blades through my rod. Then I will let the bait fall back to the bottom and repeat the process all the way back to the boat, making sure I keep the line tight to stay in touch with the lure and detect any light strikes.

When it comes to trailer hooks, I usually don't use them when fishing for fun, but I will say that if I were fishing for money, I wouldn't be caught dead without one. The main reason I forgo the trailer hook is that I like to fish the bait in very heavy cover, usually stopping the bait at times in the cover, letting it fall to entice a strike. I find it a little less frustrating not to have a trailer hook on at these times. As for a rubber trailer added to the bait, I will use this in the winter and in other slow presentation techniques; the added trailer will provide more bulk and buoyancy to the lure. When fishing the bait in a fast manner, I don't feel the need to add more bulk or buoyancy to the bait because in that circumstance I am usually looking for a reaction strike.

When fishing for cold water bass, work the bait from slow to almost a crawl; when in warm water, fish the bait fast. This might sound simple, but many times I find that people refuse to fish the bait at high speeds. Many times that fast, escaping look of a lure moving at high speed will be what attracts the fish to strike. Many times in cold water it is hard to work the lure at the slow speed needed to catch fish, but it is important to keep the bait in front of the fish as long as possible in this frigid water.

Spinner baits can be a wonderful lure to use as a search bait and will venture into many places and depths that other baits won't while searching for bass. Many times you will have fish react on the lure but not take it. This is when you want to follow up with a worm or jig. That fish is already in a heightened state and will quickly hit a follow-up lure placed in its strike zone.

Become familiar with the different styles and weights of spinner baits, and start trying them in a few more circumstances when fishing. You might find the lure does great in many applications other than just casting and winding. Learn to play with many different retrieves with the lure. Try adding as many different variations to the retrieve as you can. Try different speeds with the lure, and also try bringing the bait right through the cover that many times you are just fishing the edges of. Get to know the feel of these lures at a wide variety of depths, and learn how the vibration of the blades changes at different depths and on different types of fishing line. The more you familiarize yourself with the lure, the more you will increase the confidence you have in different situations. You will come to realize that the spinner bait has a lot more uses in catching fish than you ever thought and that it can guide you to fish you thought were out of reach for this bait. The lure can be fished shallow or deep, in clear water or muddy water; you just have to become familiar with the bait in all of these situations to gain the confidence you need to catch fish. These big fish baits should be a tool in everyone's tackle box, so never leave home without one.

Crank Baits

The two types of crank baits most commonly used are the crank bait with a lip and the lipless crank bait. Both have their advantages and are baits you need to become familiar with and use when you are out on the lake. Many people will have these lures in their tackle box but will only go to them as a last resort when all else fails. These lures are extremely productive fish-catching offerings and should be thought of as valuable tools when searching for bass. From shallow water to deep water, these baits imitate the prey fish in a lake very well and should be used any time you get a chance.

The lipless crank bait is probably the most widely used of the two, and unlike the crank bait with a lip, for which the depth is determined by the size and shape of the lip, the lipless crank bait is a sinking lure that can be fished at a wide range of depths. The bait has gained the most popularity for its ability to draw fish out of heavy grass at all times of the year. The bait can be fished over submerged vegetation at a wide range of depths and will pull the bass out as they investigate the approaching vibrations or the disturbance the bait causes as it ticks the grass. The depth at which the bait is most widely used is probably from four to six feet of water. The rattling lipless bait is reeled in close contact with the vegetation, often hanging in the grass and popped loose to entice a reaction strike. The bait excels in the standing timber also, catching the suspending bass spending time on the vertical structure. The bait can attract fish from great distances and, when the bait makes contact with the wood, can entice following bass to hit the lure with abandon. The bait works best when kept in contact with the available cover, but it will also coax strikes when the bait is kept above and around the cover. I remember a summer day on Fayette County Lake when I was catching fish coming up schooling with top water baits. I felt I was wasting much time waiting for the fish to come up and then casting to them with the top waters. Although catching these four-to-six-pound fish was a lot of fun on top, I decided to make a move to a creek channel in thirty-five feet of water with standing timber that came up to about eight feet below the surface. I knew the fish that were coming up schooling were probably holding in the trees, waiting for the shad to move by. I made a pass with the graph, and sure enough the treetops were full of bass waiting to ambush the bait. When the fish moved out on the bait, they chased the shad to the surface and were the fish I had been targeting previously. I didn't want to wait for the fish to give me a shot on their schedule; I wanted to catch them on mine. The tree line ran about a mile along the underwater creek, so I eased the boat along with the trolling motor and cast across the trees with a 1/2-oz. chrome RattleTrap. What I found was that I didn't have to wait until the fish made their presence known on the surface; they were happy to attack the crank bait while they were set up in the trees. I probably caught fifty or sixty good fish without waiting for the fish to be caught on their schedule. Many times you can make a situation work for you instead of you working for it.

The first lipless crank bait I remember fishing was the original Hot Spot. This bait when it was first introduced had no rattles or BBs inside to attract fish, but attract fish it did. I remember that the first cast I made with the bait when I was a kid produced a nice bass and had other nice fish following the lure. This gave me a lot of confidence in the lure, and I enjoyed fishing this bait for many years and always had great success with it. The one thing I notice in today's lipless baits is that they all seem to come with rattles. Sometimes I think the vibration of the bait with rattles is a well-known sound to the fish. In lakes like Sam Rayburn where the bait is a big part of an angler's arsenal, I sometimes feel the bait goes ignored because the fish have come to know that sound and vibration. Many times I will use a few different rattling baits from different manufacturers in hopes of fooling wary fish. A lot of times I do notice that the fish will hit some lures and will ignore another very similar lure altogether. The narrow profile and wobble of the bait alone will put out a lot of vibration in the water without a rattle chamber full of BBs, but I find it is almost impossible to find lipless crank baits without BBs in the stores. To overcome this, I have discovered that you can drill into the bottom of the bait and remove some or all of the BBs inside to create the sound and vibration you want. I do feel at times the fish will hit the bait with no BBs a lot better than anything else, and adjusting the BB count gives you the opportunity to more closely match the fishes' mood. The holes you make in the lure can be sealed with any waterproof glue or epoxy. Always try different variations in the baits you use; this could lead you to a more productive way to fish them when times are a little tough. Use your imagination when you use any lures, and try to come up with new ways to increase your catch.

The lipless bait also excels in deep water because the bait can sink to the fishes' depth. At times I will find suspended bass sitting over deep structure and will entice these fish to hit with these rattling baits. I will cast past the fish and let the bait sink to their level and either slowly roll the bait back to the boat at their depth, or yoyo the bait through the fish to entice a strike. Another technique that works well is to let the bait sink to the preferred depth and reel fairly fast for a few cranks of the reel handle, then stop and let the bait flutter for a few seconds, then repeat. This sometimes draws strikes when other methods simply will not; it just depends on the fishes' mood at the time. The lipless crank bait gives you the option of fishing the lure in a wide range of depths and speeds, so always take the time to try new ways of making this lure work for you. There are many ways to fish these baits, so don't hesitate to try something different with the lure that you have never tried. It might open up a whole new way to catch fish when other methods aren't producing at all.

The other popular style of crank bait is the floating or suspending lipped baits. These baits are great at producing fish over cover of any kind. Many times I fish the baits around brush or weeds to catch the most active fish before I venture in with a jig or worm. This tactic seems to produce more fish than just pulling fish from the cover with a worm or jig and spooking the suspended fish. You take advantage of two different stages of the fishes' behavior without just working the bottom of the water column and reeling fish through the suspending fish, spooking them in the process.

When working crank baits over structure, make sure the bait can get down to the fish and make contact with the bottom or cover to draw the fishes' attention. If you are going to work a hump or creek channel ledge that is ten feet of water on the top, use a crank bait that will dive deeper than the depth you are fishing, and adjust the depth needed by changing speed or line size. This allows you to put the bait in the fish's face. When the lure encounters a definite collision with a piece of cover, pause the bait immediately and let it float up or suspend. This will trigger a strike from a sluggish fish that thinks it is going to take advantage of a stunned bait fish. Bass are very opportunistic feeders, and a bass won't hesitate to take advantage of a bait fish's unfortunate collision with an object. An erratic retrieve with this bait will always produce more strikes than just reeling the bait steadily back to the boat. Slow down and speed up with the lure at times, and stop and start with the lure to give the bait an erratic motion when reeling it back to the boat. Try to make the bait stand out from the other bait fish in the area. Fish will take any opportunity to take advantage of a wounded bait fish, even when the fish are not active, so always try to give the bait an erratic action to attract the interest of a nearby bass. Making contact with standing timber, dock pilings, or other hard structure will often entice a strike when just reeling the bait past the structure will not. Use the natural trigger instincts a bass possesses to draw more strikes from slightly more inactive fish; it will pay off in the long run with more hits.

Crank baits are a valuable tool and can be used for a wide array of situations; it would take a while to cover them all, so I will leave it at the techniques we have covered. Try to use these baits a little more and experiment with them more often in different scenarios to become more versatile and confident with them.

Top Water Lures

When talking about these baits, I guess the place to start is with the different types. There are floating soft plastic baits, buzz baits, poppers, the propeller type, walking baits, and my favorite, the quiet top waters.

The most popular top waters are probably buzz baits and the walking baits. The walking baits have been a favorite of top water fisherman for many years. Not only do they entice lurking bass with their fleeing prey appearance, but they also resemble a wounded bait fish spending its last efforts for survival moving across the top of the water. Walking the dog with the bait gives the angler constant activity and keeps him involved while working the bait, unlike some slower pop and wait methods that can seem a little slow for the angler at times. This tactic gives you the ability to cover more water and move through areas that don't produce a little more quickly. The bait excels when targeting fish in deep water that are attacking schools of bait fish on the surface. The bait resembles wounded prey trying to escape the melee, triggering a response from a bass trying to catch an easy meal before it's out of the area. The size of the bait can be very important; try to match as closely as possible the size of bait fish in the area. When blind casting for big bass near the shoreline or over cover, a fairly large bait will sometimes draw more strikes. Big bass seem to have a liking for big things that move across the surface of the water. Varying the retrieve, rather than just maintaining an even pace back to the boat, will sometimes make a fish react to the bait. At times a pause in the lure on the retrieve can entice that following fish to go into action. While the natural colors work well, a baby bass pattern or a frog pattern work well on the walking baits.

The buzz bait is a top water that really isn't made to mimic a bait fish, but rather it is designed to mimic some of the other land-born creatures that make their way into the fishes' domain. This bait seems to draw more strikes from larger fish than do most top waters. The older fish have at times in their lives encountered these land-based creatures and are very willing to enjoy the very filling opportunity again. They know that land-based prey is at a distinct disadvantage when it enters the water, and a big bass will take full advantage of this fact. Buzz baits can be fished in the heaviest grass and cover you wish to fish. The upturned hook and the way the bait rides on the top will clear most obstacles with ease. The one thing that seems to matter a lot is the length of the hook shaft. A lure with a shaft that sticks out past the hook at least two inches or so will increase the number of hook ups. My brother-in-law Gary learned this the hard way. After Gibbons Creek Reservoir opened, the lake had kind of a bad reputation that seemed to make the rounds. I had been tearing up the lake with big fish and was surprised when Gary mentioned the unfounded news he had heard. I assured him that nothing could be farther from the truth and he should come up and see for himself. Gary did make it up, so we headed out on this new lake to work buzz baits in the timber along a creek. I had been doing really well on the top waters and wanted Gary to experience what I had been enjoying. Needless to say, we caught big fish on buzz baits all day, and he had a trip to remember. The one thing I remember is that at one point I saw him bring his bait by a bush four times with a big fish blowing up on it every time. Before the fourth cast I told him that if he didn't hook the fish that cast, I would snag it for him. Then, after he missed the fish, I flipped over by the bush and hooked the nice fish. He couldn't believe it and said he had gotten him ready for me. I told him that wasn't the case and showed him that the bait I was throwing had a shaft that stuck out past the hook about an inch-and-a-half farther than his. He said he never even thought about that and, after seeing that his hook only stuck out past the blade about an inch, quickly changed to a different buzz bait. The little things can really matter sometimes.

The buzz bait can be fished from sunup to sundown with effectiveness, I think much more than other types of top waters can. I have had success with the bait in two feet of water in the middle of the afternoon during the summer. There is something about the action that really draws strikes from inactive fish when many other types of top water baits will not. I think it has to do with the fact that the baits resemble the land-based prey mentioned earlier, and the fish don't want to miss a chance at a good meal. Give a buzz bait a try the next time you are in the mood for a heart-stopping explosion from a big bass, but make sure your heart can take it. This bait is truly not for the faint of heart.

Propeller and popping baits are very similar, and you will have to experiment at times to see which works better. Both will work well on schooling fish, but there are poppers that seem to cast a little farther, and this really helps when targeting schooling fish. Both baits work great in a slow presentation. Cast either out and let it settle; give the bait a pop or two and let it settle until all the rings die down before repeating the process. The propeller bait gives out a swishing sound as you pop it, and the popper, like the name says, gives a nice pop. You will have to try both to see which works best at a given time. When fish are active they will explode on the bait as if they hadn't eaten in weeks. It is a very exciting way to fish, but it is a little slow for the fast-paced fisherman when the fish aren't very active, so many fishermen will tend to fish the lure at sunup and sundown when the fish are the most active and can be attracted to the top in the low light conditions. I have always enjoyed fishing the lure in the last hour of daylight on Lake Sam Rayburn when the fish move out of the shoreline bushes to feed. I catch some really good fish by taking advantage of this afternoon migration the bass make.

The last group of top water baits I will cover is the soft plastic and quiet baits. The term quiet bait is not a commonly used term for top waters anymore, but I feel they have an important part to play in the top water arsenal. A bait that I have always had a great deal of confidence in, and a great deal of success with, is a top water bait I can't find any more called a Carrot Top, made by Cordell, I believe. This bait is shaped like a carrot, and at rest the head sticks out of the water while the back end drops below the surface. I have always used the chrome version of the bait and have never seen a reason to change. When the bait is popped, it quietly dives below the surface and quietly comes to rest. It seems to drive fish crazy; I love it.

In the mid-seventies, I went on a trip to Toledo Bend Reservoir with a friend's family. Because of my love of fishing, I planned to rent a small boat and head out on the lake and catch some good fish. After my arrival, I went to rent a small aluminum boat and head out for some fishing. The operator of the bait camp informed me that the fishing had been really slow for a while and that because of the summer heat he didn't expect it to get any better. I informed him I was planning to catch some good fish on top water, and all I got in return was a hearty laugh from the marina operator. He told me that all the fish that were being caught were in fifteen feet of water or deeper, then laughed again. He said, "You're just not going to have much luck on top." I smiled as I got the little rented boat ready and headed out for some top water fishing. My friend was not a fisherman at all, but he wanted to head out with me to soak up some sun. I looked around the lake a little and decided on the back of a large cove that had a huge area matted with hydrilla, with small open pockets where the hydrilla didn't quite make it to the top. My first cast, to one of the shallow depressions in the grass, was met with a tremendous explosion, and a four-pound fish was brought to the boat after a stubborn fight. Who was laughing then! I was keeping fish for a big fish fry, so I put the bass on the stringer and sought out the next pocket. The next cast was greeted by a nice two- pound fish that made its way onto the stringer. These fish were so active they would spend several minutes jumping out of the water after they were put on the stringer. The attacks on my Carrot Top were ferocious, and many times I could see several other wakes heading for the bait, but they were usually too late. The limit was fifteen bass, and it took me about an hour and a half to fill the stringer. The stringer was loaded with bass from two to five pounds, most of them in the three- to four-pound class. It was a beautiful stringer of fish for a young teenager. I had had a great time, so I headed into the dock to clean my fish and get ready for the next day of fishing. As I pulled up by the little house that we were renting, I lifted the stringer of fish up out of the boat and put it back in the water. This was not missed by many. Other fishermen were sitting around talking about how slow the fishing was, when this snot-nosed kid dared to bring in a stringer like that. I stowed my equipment, not paying any attention to the gathering mob, but when I returned to take my fish to the cleaning table, I was amazed at the people gawking at my fish—they were only fish! I threw the stringer on the cleaning table and was greeted by the marina operator, who handed me a nice cold soda. He smiled and said, "I guess you're going to tell me you caught these fish on top waters." I smiled and said, "Yes sir, that's what I wanted to do. I love top water fishing." As he walked away I heard him mumble, "So don't tell me how you caught them." I think it was hard for people to believe I had caught these fish in shallow water on top waters in the heat of the summer, all but one older gentleman that was staying in the house next door to ours. He congratulated me on my top water catch and said that he was amazed at my great success. For the next three days I experienced some great top water fishing for big bass, catching fish after fish, and I seemed to have to whole lake to myself, with the exception of one older gentleman whom I gladly told to follow me to where I had been enjoying the action. It surprised me that he was the only one who asked where and how I was fishing. We both literally hammered the fish, and before I left the lake to head home, he told me with a satisfied smile on his face that he had just enjoyed the best top water fishing of his life, and he really appreciated my showing him what I was doing. I told him the pleasure was all mine, and it was a pleasure; he was a great guy.

When you go fishing, you have to make a plan and decide what you want to do. Make your plan work for you, and never let what anyone says change the course you have set for yourself. Know you have made the right choices for the fishing you enjoy.

The other quiet top waters are the soft plastics. The advantage of these lures is that they can be fished at a very slow pace, unlike the buzz bait that has to remain at a steady pace to avoid hang ups. The soft plastics are mainly the frogs, rats, and floating lizards. They can be fished in the heaviest of cover as slowly as you wish to fish them. You can keep the bait in front of the bass for as long as it takes to entice her to react on the offering.

The hollow-body frogs and rats, along with the solid-body frogs, have become very popular for fishing the matted vegetation in grass-filled lakes. The bait can be worked over the little openings and depressions at a slow speed, allowing the fish to find the bait through the mat. There are definite high percentage locations when fishing the mat. When you find a pattern, make sure to repeat that pattern throughout the mat. The fish will hold on certain features of the mat, and the key is to locate that feature to avoid blind casting to unproductive water. Sometimes you will find the fish far back in the mat, and sometimes you will find them on the outer edges near deeper water. The key is to quickly put together a pattern. When you catch a few good fish, let that give you an idea of the high percentage spots to key on. Pay attention to all areas of the mats; many times you can see bait flipping out of the water at certain areas in the mat. This will give you an idea where to direct your cast. There are two opposite approaches that seem to work well in the matted grass. One is to bring the bait near all of the open areas you can find, and the other is to bring the bait near the heaviest clumps in the mat. Once you find which is the most productive, you will have an idea of the key areas to target.

A top water lure I love is the floating lizard. I can't say how many fish I have pulled from heavy cover on the flip tail floating lizard. Although I don't think the bait is made anymore, there are many substitutes on the market that will work. I will fish the lizard in and around grass, but I prefer to fish it in wood. Areas that are hard to reach, loaded with lay downs with scattered grass, are ideal for this bait. It doesn't take much of a hole in the cover to get an explosive strike from a lurking bass. Put forth a little effort to get yourself into areas that most other fisherman won't spend the time to find. When you put yourself in these areas, you can offer the bait to bass that seldom see pressure, and these bass will quickly react on a floating lizard. They think this prey has ventured into their tight location by mistake, and they will gladly take advantage of that mistake.

Top waters aren't just for early and late situations. They can be fished throughout the day to get non-active fish to hit. They really are amazing for the way fish will react to them. Fish will always take advantage of prey that is at a disadvantage, and nothing, to the fish's view, is at more of a disadvantage than a sure meal on top of the water where it can't see the bass coming.

Jigging Spoons

This is a lure you need to become familiar with. No other bait gives you more direct contact with the bass. The jigging spoon can be dropped right on top of the fish when they are located, or the lure can be cast out and jigged back to the boat when you are searching for bass on deep water structure. I have a lot of confidence in the lures because of the number of good fish I have caught on them over the years. I became quite dependant on the lures for years while fishing on Lake Conroe. In the late seventies and early eighties, the grass carp that were introduced into the lake quickly made the lake void of all vegetation. Because of this, I had to get to know this lake all over again. The advantage of fishing the grass, along with the edges it created, was gone, and I had to find new structure to fish. I would cover the lake from side to side, finding every drop off, creek channel, ridge, hump, and pond dam I could find. When I found these areas, I would drop a spoon on the fish while I moved around the structure with my depth finder, becoming familiar with the ins and outs of the sweet spot. Many times when I found a good area of structure I would fan cast with a spoon or Little George, to find the spots that held the fish. This allowed me to cover more water and then move in to investigate the area when a fish was caught. It seems now I know the lay of the bottom of the lake as if it had no water in it. I can attribute this deep learning to the fact that I covered the lake with my electronics and fished the areas that I found with a jigging spoon. This allowed me to learn the areas in more depth while I was actually fishing.

When you locate fish on an area of structure, simply toss out a buoy and return to the spot and pick it apart with the spoon. For bass, a small hop off of the bottom seems to produce better, and remember to always let the bait fall back to the bottom on the fall. The fish will hit the bait on the fall, and the strike is hard to detect at times. As you pop the rod up for your next hop, be ready to set the hook if you feel resistance. It is important to set the hook well because of the ease with which a fish can throw this heavy bait. You will find, after you start to become more efficient at this tactic, that the quality of bass you catch while jigging makes the time you have spent on your electronics well worth it.

Don't be afraid of using a jigging spoon over heavy cover. You will get hung up fairly regularly, but as you do this more and more, you will learn to detect the difference between brush and a fish. The weight of the spoon makes it fairly easy to wiggle the bait free on a loose line. There is no other lure that so closely resembles a wounded shad as a jigging spoon, so anywhere that bass feed on schools of shad is a great location to search for hungry bass with this lure. This is the ultimate search bait, not for finding the fish but for finding the sweet spots that hold fish.

Remember that these little lures really help you become familiar with the areas you are fishing. When you watch your electronics as you fish underwater structure, you will start to notice the little changes in the bottom's makeup that will attract the bass to that spot on the structure. It is a great tool that allows you to catch fish while letting you learn more about the structure you are fishing.

Jigging for Bass

Swim Baits

Swim baits have been around for a long time, although it seems that just recently these baits have become more popular than ever. Years back I would use a large paddle tail type soft plastic on a half-ounce jig head to serve as what is now called a swim bait. Nowadays there are a lot of finely manufactured swim baits on the market, many very closely resembling the prey the bass feed on. Some of these baits are a little pricey, but they are well worth the cost because of the realism they bring to enticing wary bass and also the quality and quantity of the hooks they have made into the bait. These new swim baits impart many new innovations to attract bass. Many use a jointed body that uses water flow to provide a realistic swimming motion, and others use soft plastics to create a natural swimming motion by the type of tail molded into the bait. I have always used the swim bait in the lower part of the water column up to the mid depths for suspended fish, but the bait has become popular for enticing fish to the top, making a big bass think she is taking advantage of a wounded bait fish. Whichever depth you decide to work the bait, there are several retrieves to be tried in order to find the one that the fish react to the best.

The way I usually use the swim bait is to locate some deep structure that is holding plenty of bait, along with bass waiting to make an easy meal of the balled-up shad. I will cast the bait out and let it sink to the appropriate depth and start my retrieve. I find there are two ways that work best to entice a strike. The first and the one I use the most is to crank the handle of the reel very fast about six to eight times and then pause to let the bait settle back to the preferred depth. I will repeat this all the way back to the boat, making sure the bait is staying at the prime depth for as long as possible. The strikes will occur when the bait is on the fall, so paying attention to your line is very important. Most times, you can feel the hit by keeping a slightly tight line, but always be aware of any tension on the line when you start to reel again. If you feel resistance, set the hook as soon as you detect any change in the feel of your retrieve. This method is the one that I feel attracts the most attention from the bass holding on schools of shad. The other method I use is to let the bait fall to the preferred depth and give the bait hard jerks with the rod and let the bait fall. This hopping tactic seems to work best when bass are really running the shad, and larger fish from below are taking advantage of the wounded stragglers.

When bass are less active, I will sometimes slow roll the swim bait through the prime depths. This will look more attractive to the less active fish. The bait will stand out from the grouped up shad, and a waiting bass can't resist the odd fish that stands out from the rest. This slow rolling technique seems to work best when fishing the bait very shallow, also. The key is to get the bait to create a wake on the surface of the water; this best imitates wounded and dying prey. When fish aren't very active, I will pause the bait at times, trying to trigger a following fish. Other times I will slow roll the lure about half way to the boat, keeping the bait on the top, then increase the speed to try to get a following fish to hit by making it react on what it thinks is an injured bait fish trying to leave the area.

The term "swim bait" really covers quite a few baits in your tackle box. The finesse type minnow baits, such as the bass assassin style baits, are really swim baits. These baits are usually fished weightless and are given their action by the movement of the rod tip. They will move from side to side, and up and down, staying in the fishes' strike zone longer than other weighted swim baits. This can really mimic a wounded bait fish and drive a bass crazy. Remember that a bass will always try to take advantage of any prey it thinks is at a disadvantage.

Whichever tactic or style of swim bait you choose, these baits give you the opportunity to work the bait as you wish with the action you give your rod, while letting you put the realistically swimming bait in front of a bass's nose. Use of a swim bait is a much more subtle approach while searching a deep water structure to find the sweet spots. The bait can be manipulated with your rod and reel to match the mood of the bass. From top to bottom, swim baits are just another valuable tool to add to your fishing arsenal. Many times the price of realistic looking swim baits is well worth paying, especially when trying to entice the very wary upper end bass we all want to catch.

Fishing on the Bottom

The two lures that are used the most when covering the bottom are the soft plastic worm or lizard and the skirted jig. Both work well when fished along the bottom, but the choice is usually based on which one you have the most confidence with. The worm's slender profile gives off less vibration while attracting bass with its visual appeal. A worm resembles much of the natural prey that a bass targets, and for many years these lures have received a lot of attention from hungry bass. The worm can be fished at any depth you wish, and the action of the worm and the speed of the fall can be changed by adjusting the amount of weight you select. The jig, on the other hand, gives off a lot more vibration and is mainly intended to resemble a crawfish, a highly preferred meal for the bass. It can be fished in any cover and excels in thick cover, where its bulk and vibration make it easier for the embedded bass to find. The rate of fall in this bait is controlled by the weight of the head and the bulk of the trailer you choose. The vibration of the bait can be enhanced by adding a rattle chamber to the jig, and I will usually not throw a jig without one. I feel the rattle gives me a lot more hits than I would get without it.

The key to either of these baits is to put them in high percentage places along the lake bottom; this means you need to fish them in the area or the cover that holds fish. These baits are made to entice strikes in cover. To increase the amount of attention from a bass, fish the baits in grass, brush, timber, or rocks—places where the bass live. These are slow presentation baits, so fish them in the spots that will best eliminate wasted time. Key on the areas a bass will set up on to attack its prey. When one of these bottom bouncing morsels comes venturing by, a bass can't resist. Fishing a worm or jig can be mind numbing when you are not fishing where the bass are. This makes for a long day.

In fishing with worms, there are three set ups that are the most widely used by anglers. The first is the Texas rigged worm.

This is the most widely used set up and can be fished in a wide array of covers. The line is run through a cone slip sinker, and a worm hook is tied to the line so the weight moves freely and will settle on the head of the worm when retrieved. In flipping situations or when fishing heavy brush, the weight can be pegged to the line to keep the weight from sliding up the line. This helps you stay in contact with the bait as you work it through the heavy cover. You should select the size of the hook to match the worm you have selected. Stay with the largest hook that will work with the worm; this will ensure better hooking characteristics. A wide gap hook will make sure the rubber of the worm doesn't interfere with getting a proper hook up; sometimes the rubber will fill the gap of the hook and restrict the depth of penetration. This style of set up can be fished in the widest variety of covers and can be worked in a seductive manner to attract the most finicky bass. In the history of bass fishing, the Texas rigged worm has probably accounted for more big bass being caught than any other lure. Using this lure is a tactic you need to become very familiar with, a tactic you need to practice in every depth and cover you can find. Becoming proficient with the Texas rigged worm will put many good fish in the boat when other methods won't. It just takes time to become aware of every little feel that goes on with the set up.

The next most widely used set up for worm fishing is the Carolina rig. In this rig, the weight is set up the line from the hook anywhere from one foot to four feet, depending on the cover being fished. The most popular distance is eighteen to twenty-four inches above the hook's tag line; this will work in most circumstances. The weight is usually separated from the tag line by a barrel swivel. The weight will be above the swivel, and often one or two plastic beads will be added to create noise. Many times I have left this set up just sitting in one spot and shaken my rod tip to create noise with the bait; this can attract fish and really seems to turn the fish on at times. On many occasions, I have had fish hit the weight itself because of the action and noise of the sinker. The advantage of this set up is that you can fish a heavy weight, allowing the bait to get to the bottom more quickly. Also, the bait can be worked productively more quickly, allowing you to cover more water in your search for fish. The Carolina rig is the search bait of the worm family. Sometimes the hits are a little harder to detect than with a Texas rigged worm, and the line can have a lot of slack when the strike is detected. When you feel a strike, it is best to reel down on the fish before you set the hook. A big bonus to using a Carolina rig is that you can use a floating worm to bring the bait off the bottom, making it more attractive to a bass. Whichever morsel you choose to put on the hook, you need to fish this rig whenever possible to become more in tune with the hits. Don't worry, the fish seem to hold on the bait for a while most of the time, but learn to detect the subtle strikes for the fishes' sake; they can easily swallow the hook.

The last set up to cover is what is now called the drop shot rig. Years back I referred to the rig as a dancing worm rig. This finesse rig has gained in popularity over the last few years. It gives the angler the ability to keep a small worm or bait fish imitation in the strike zone longer. This dancing worm tactic will coax inactive fish into striking by sheer irritation. A fish will look at the bait for a while and slowly near the bait as it tries to figure it out then, out of annoyance, will attack the bait for invading its space. The rig is set up by tying a 1/8th- to 1/2-ounce wire tie weight to the end of the line, then looping a small wire live bait hook about one to two feet above the weight. The weight will stay in contact with the bottom, and the worm can be danced by very slightly popping your rod tip; this will drive the bass crazy. A four-inch worm or a small minnow-shaped soft plastic is the most popular for this technique. The hit can be slight at times, so stay in contact with the bait and set the hook when you feel any resistance. Many times the fish will slowly move in on the bait and just take a nip, so be aware of any changes you feel.

When it comes to jigs, anything goes. Deep water, shallow water, thick weeds or brush, and rocks—this bait will cover them all. You can hop the bait on the bottom like a worm or slowly swim the bait back to you, staying in contact with the cover and pausing at times to let the jig investigate any holes. There are times when spinner bait puts out a little too much vibration for the fishes' liking. Many times bringing a jig through the same area just as you would work a spinner bait will entice these finicky fish to hit.

The jig has always been one of my favorite lures for flipping into heavy cover and will draw vicious strikes from fish as it moves into their area. In clear water lakes where crawfish are a staple, the jig is hard to beat along these lakes rocky shorelines. A heavy jig, one ounce or so, is also a great bait for pulling big fish off deep water structure.

I find that many anglers don't have enough confidence in a jig to stick it out when fishing them, but a few instances of seeing what the bait can really do will cure them of any doubt. The jig is a great big bass bait, so give these lures a try and see what they can do for you. Use dark in off-colored water and natural in clear water. I usually prefer to fish a jig in stained to off-colored water, but I have found that the bait will attract good fish in clear water when a natural crawfish color is used. I will often put the bait in the heaviest cover available, in the dirtiest water around, and enjoy some good fishing for solid fish that most anglers will pass up. The muddiest of water will usually send other fishermen looking for clearer water, but I have found that fish will feed heavily in these conditions, so do be afraid to try it.

We have covered a few baits, and the key to getting the most out of them is to visualize what the fish are doing and select the best bait for that situation. If the fish aren't reacting the way you want to the bait you choose, don't hesitate: change to a bait you feel might draw a better response from the fish. Use that computer we call the mind to eliminate the baits that don't fit the situation, and put on the baits that give you the best opportunity to put fish in the boat.

No other bait puts you in more contact with the fish than these bottom bouncing lures.

The Best Way to Spook Bass

Spooking the bass we chase is probably something most people don't give a lot of thought, but it is something that is done a lot more than anglers think. Fishermen fish the way they always have, blindly moving through an area without noticing that their actions can be affecting the outcome of their fishing. Most anglers will never know what could have been if they had taken a little more care in how they approached the area that they are fishing. When a fisherman is fishing for a bass that is set up on its bed, this might be the only time he tries to be quiet and restrict his movements in order to avoid spooking that wary bass. The fact is, we should pay a lot more attention to our movements and a lot more attention to the sounds we make while moving around in the boat. Think ahead before you enter an area to fish: how close is close? The majority of the fish that are caught in shallow water are on the small side, though this is not to say that there are not some real heavyweights lurking in the shallows at times. Shallow water does hold a good number of juvenile fish all year long, but many times the older fish that are there are a little more wary than the younger fish and have already been made aware of your presence. There has probably been at least one time when you were out fishing that you have spooked a big fish out of the area without even knowing she was there. Try to think before you move into an area to fish, and take steps to avoid spooking any mature fish, driving them out of that area before you even have a chance to catch them.

When approaching older fish in shallow water, you have to take into consideration your overall profile in the boat. By this I mean that just standing in the boat on the same side you are fishing on will many times spook wary fish with the sudden movement of your cast. While standing in the boat while you operate the trolling motor is the best way to stay focused and in tune with what you are doing, more often than not your movements will not go unnoticed by the shallow bass in the area. Sometimes sitting is a much more stealthy way to approach shallow fish, or even standing in a lower portion of the boat away from the side you are fishing on will give you a much lower profile. Creating a lower profile in the boat will make it harder for a fish to pick up your movements. The sudden movement of casting or just moving around in the boat will not go undetected by the shallow fish in the area, so take care how you approach these shallow fish; a lower profile will give you an edge in moving in on shallow bass.

When fishing in stained or off-colored water, or when fishing in deeper water, the movements you make aren't nearly as critical. However, in these situations, you need to pay attention to the sounds you make almost as much as you do in shallow water. The sound of closing your tackle box too loudly or the sound of a bass splashing around in the live well will usually alert the bass in the area that something isn't quite right, and this can be enough to shut the feeding activity off in the area that you are fishing. Be sure to make an effort to lessen your profile in the boat, along with eliminating any boat noise you can, including paying attention to the wave slaps against the side of the boat. Feel free to cut up and laugh all you want above the water level, but any sound you transmit through the hull of your boat will be detected by the bass in the area, and these sounds have a tendency to carry a long way out from the boat. Remember, the slightest sound that a fish is not used to hearing will quickly alert the fish in the area to your presence.

When we catch a good fish it is hard not to celebrate a little. A few high fives and congratulations are expected. Many times after we catch a big fish we forget that other good fish could be in the area, and we just move around the boat not paying any attention at all to the sounds we are making. Grabbing the camera to capture the moment or just closing a hatch too loudly may be all it takes to send the other fish in the vicinity heading for the deep. Next time you're out on the water, try to notice all the noises you make when moving around the boat, and try to figure out ways you can be a little quieter when doing the things you must do in your boat. This small change could mean catching that fish of a lifetime. Bass can be extremely wary at times, so we have to do everything we can to keep them from spooking. Sound travels a long way under water at a very fast speed, so to catch big fish in shallow water, we have to do everything we can to avoid alerting them to our presence.

The Mental Approach to Fishing

As I said in my book on fishing the Texas coast (*Fishing Magic: The Texas Coast*), I can't stress enough how important the mental part of fishing really is and how it relates to the outcome of every day you spend on the lake. Everything I have talked about so far in this book is not nearly as important as the mindset you have while you are fishing. If you don't have the proper mindset when you fish, you will never reach the level you want to reach as an angler. I learned from an early age that when I went fishing I had to visualize what the outcome of my fishing trip was going to be, and more often than not that's just how the trip ended up. I always had a positive feeling before I went fishing about what I was going to accomplish on the lake, and many times I told others how my trip was going to turn out. I have always been amazed at how my fishing trips turn out to be very close to how I imagined them to be. From the beginning, my father was always amazed by this and would say that if he filled a bathtub with water I could catch a fish out of it. To tell the truth, it is the fact that I know I'm going to have a certain outcome when I go fishing, and that I use this to achieve my goals, that makes me the fisherman I have always been. You have to create your own luck when fishing. It works, and I believe this above all else. It is my positive outlook when I am fishing that gives me the incredible angling success I have enjoyed my whole life.

I don't know if you have ever heard the term The Law of Attraction, but it is a proven force of nature and a force that can be harnessed for your advantage when fishing. If you visualize the outcome of your fishing day, more than likely that is the outcome you will have. Any doubts or negative thoughts you let enter your mind are going to affect the outcome of your fishing that day. You might have trouble with the traffic at the boat ramp, or maybe trouble with your boat itself. Letting these things bother you in any way will ruin your day if you can't get back on top of it. Practice telling yourself that these things are all part of the sport you love, and learn to let the little setbacks roll off your back. You will run into things that frustrate you at times, so try to learn some techniques that will turn your negative mood around; they will really help. First, before you get to the boat ramp, visualize how things are going to go ahead of time. Already know the crowds won't bother you, and any problems with the boat will be fixed quickly. Try not to let these things catch you off guard and surprise you; this will make it easier to work through these inconveniences. You will find that most of the time you avoid any problems by just creating a certain start to the day in your head and calmly going through the game plan. When things start to get a little out of hand and you find yourself starting to get a little frustrated, find something to think about that will help you get yourself above the frustration. Maybe play out in your mind a mental scene of you landing a big bass and letting her go to fight another day. Really see yourself holding the fish, and see yourself actually slipping her back into the water. Keep replaying this scene over and over in your mind until the frustration starts to leave. Whatever nice scene you can come up with will work, and always use this same scene to put you back into the proper state of mind.

There is no greater tool for the tournament angler than his mindset. You can see by the fishermen that are always at the top of each tournament which ones have learned to harness their mental power, and use it for what it's made for, to create the outcome they wish. There are tournament bass fishermen that can start off each tournament doing great, but when things start to go wrong, they will dwell on those little things and slowly slip from the upper tier. These anglers probably wonder why they can get so close but never finish number one. The reason is their mental approach; they can't control their mindset while in the heat of battle. They let outside influences start to enter the plan they have set, and this will always affect their outcome. The winners know before each tournament that they are going to catch good fish; they just have to locate the area and find the techniques that will put these fish in the boat. It's that easy. All of the pro anglers have the mechanics and the knowhow; it's the ones who have learned to harness the power of positive thinking that move to the top. A fisherman who can't make that final push to finish at the top is a fisherman who can't control the outside influences he or she encounters. The mental pressure of just fishing these bass tournaments is incredible. The pressure they put on themselves is enough to break many of the competitors. It is the ones who can compete with themselves while competing with the other anglers who move to the top. Tournament fishing is not for everyone, and I will say one thing for sure: it's only for the strong of mind. The stress a tournament places on an angler is incredible, and many anglers can't take that pressure for very long. The anglers who fish these circuits for a long period of time should be respected for their mental fortitude.

Learn to start every fishing trip by visualizing how your day is going to be. Know you will catch plenty of fish and have a great day on the lake while doing it. If you find yourself starting to doubt how the day will be, find something else to visualize other than the bad feelings in order to turn your negative thoughts around. Maybe visualize the fish moving in on your bait, or maybe see yourself landing a big fish. Whatever it is that you wish to visualize, do it; your day depends on it.

Try to always create good vibes while fishing, especially when fishing with others, and be thankful that you are doing what you love. This will keep you in a positive state of mind and will help the other people in your boat have a good fishing day, too. But if you find yourself losing that positive feeling, find something good to start visualizing until the good things start to happen again. And if you notice someone else starting to have a tough time, quickly do something to help them change their frame of mind.

I have fished with many people over the years who could find anything at all to ruin their day on the lake, most of the time without their even realizing it. I have heard many excuses along the way. Some people even say certain things are a jinx. Trust me, there is no such thing. If you think something will jinx you, it will, not because it's a jinx but because you made it so in your mind, and your expectations came true. You have to remember that your thoughts will become a fact, good or bad, so be careful what you ask for. You have to create the outcome you desire in your mind, and not stray from it in any way, and trust me, it will happen. It's a power you should be proud of possessing, so use it to create the success you want to have when out on the lake. You also have the power to hurt the outcome of the day with negative thoughts. What you think is going to happen will, good or bad. Another thing to remember is that if things seem to slow down in a certain area, don't fight it; just move to a new area and make the good things start to happen there, too.

We talked earlier about keeping a fishing log that you fill in *before* you go fishing. Write down how the day is going to be, and what kind of success you are going to have. When you write things down, they seem to have a little more power in your mind. You will start to find out, when you go back and read what you had planned, that the day ended up very close to the day you wanted. This is a good tool to use in helping you start to visualize your trips. It is so important to visualize the day you will have. There is nothing else that will put more fish in your boat than a positive visualization of the day ahead. I am serious about this; there is nothing that will aid you more in catching fish.

Make several plans for the day's fishing, depending on the prevailing conditions. Know that all of them are good plans and that whatever the day throws at you, any of the plans will produce fish. Never hesitate in making a move to another location if the urge strikes; react on these thoughts, and move to that location and create the fishing you want. Don't let what others tell you affect your fishing plans. What they have created for themselves might not work for you. Fishing is very personal, so create a day for you. If you want to catch fish in a certain place, on particular baits, then do it. Nobody can affect the day you plan for yourself. The mind is by far the most powerful asset you have when fishing, so use it for all that it is worth. Know you will have a great day, and you will. The mind is a terrible thing to waste, so don't!

In Closing

There is no better way to describe the art of fishing than with the word "desire." The desire to have a good day, the desire for the bite, and the desire of the fight are all deep-seated desires. Sometimes it might be the desire for solitude or the desire to be out in all of nature's glory. However you look at it, fishing is desire. After making your plan to approach your day of fishing, you have a strong desire to have that plan work the way you want it to. Don't let anything chase that desire from your heart while you work through the plan of the day. Remember that it is so easy to let doubts creep in and wear away at the desire you possess. The desire to make your plan work is paramount, so don't weaken your drive to make it happen. The desire to bring success to your fishing trips can be truly magical. Fishing magic might sound like an odd term to describe the bounty that confidence brings, but learning to use all that confidence has to offer truly is magic.

When the fishing bug does bite you and won't let go, you have just been infected with a wonderful sickness—a sickness that at times can make you embarrassed to admit how much it consumes you. Once you have contracted this sickness, you don't need to worry about the outcome; there is a great treatment program for this bug. The treatment is to fish!

You might feel a lot of what I have said about the laws of attraction while fishing is a load; I feel it is more likely a load of fish. I feel it is some of the most important information that you can learn to help you increase the number of fish you catch. All of the newest lures in all of the newest colors and actions along with the most high-tech tackle and electronics will not bring the success you want as much as learning to use your confidence while fishing. Please try to start to give these little things a try when out on your next fishing trip. I think you will definitely see a difference in the outcome of those trips.

Another important aspect of your fishing trips to consider is the time you spend getting to know the fish you are chasing. It is very hard at times to make yourself spend the time it takes to find the most productive areas with your electronics. You know there are fish out there waiting to be caught, so you can't stand it; you make for the first fishy looking spot and start the day prematurely. This is something that you need to fight until you know you have found some key areas to search for bass.

There is the saying that ten percent of the fishermen catch ninety percent of the fish; being part of that ten percent is sometimes just a matter of noticing the small clues that nature has to offer or picking up the signs that will lead you to the basses' travel routes and pit stops.

Add the attraction power of your mind any time you can while fishing, and become the angler you want to be. Don't listen to what the masses think; do what you want to do to enjoy your fishing. You can create the outcome you want just by conditioning yourself to do so. Good luck and good fishing, and always do it your way.

Made in the USA
Columbia, SC
04 July 2017